# Session Notes

# N O T E B O O K

## PERSONAL DETAILS

Name : ..........................................................................................

Address : ......................................................................................

Email : .........................................................................................

Phone Number : ...........................................................................

Fax Number  : ..............................................................................

Log Start Date : ...........................................................................

Log Book Number : ......................................................................

# ADDITIONAL INFORMATION

| Date | Client Name | Contact No | Session No | Page# | Notes |
|------|-------------|------------|------------|-------|-------|
|      |             |            |            |       |       |
|      |             |            |            |       |       |
|      |             |            |            |       |       |
|      |             |            |            |       |       |
|      |             |            |            |       |       |
|      |             |            |            |       |       |
|      |             |            |            |       |       |
|      |             |            |            |       |       |
|      |             |            |            |       |       |
|      |             |            |            |       |       |
|      |             |            |            |       |       |
|      |             |            |            |       |       |
|      |             |            |            |       |       |
|      |             |            |            |       |       |
|      |             |            |            |       |       |
|      |             |            |            |       |       |
|      |             |            |            |       |       |
|      |             |            |            |       |       |
|      |             |            |            |       |       |

| Date | Client Name | Contact No | Session No | Page# | Notes |
|------|-------------|------------|------------|-------|-------|
|      |             |            |            |       |       |
|      |             |            |            |       |       |
|      |             |            |            |       |       |
|      |             |            |            |       |       |
|      |             |            |            |       |       |
|      |             |            |            |       |       |
|      |             |            |            |       |       |
|      |             |            |            |       |       |
|      |             |            |            |       |       |
|      |             |            |            |       |       |
|      |             |            |            |       |       |
|      |             |            |            |       |       |
|      |             |            |            |       |       |
|      |             |            |            |       |       |
|      |             |            |            |       |       |
|      |             |            |            |       |       |
|      |             |            |            |       |       |
|      |             |            |            |       |       |
|      |             |            |            |       |       |

| Date | Client Name | Contact No | Session No | Page# | Notes |
|------|-------------|------------|------------|-------|-------|
|      |             |            |            |       |       |
|      |             |            |            |       |       |
|      |             |            |            |       |       |
|      |             |            |            |       |       |
|      |             |            |            |       |       |
|      |             |            |            |       |       |
|      |             |            |            |       |       |
|      |             |            |            |       |       |
|      |             |            |            |       |       |
|      |             |            |            |       |       |
|      |             |            |            |       |       |
|      |             |            |            |       |       |
|      |             |            |            |       |       |
|      |             |            |            |       |       |
|      |             |            |            |       |       |
|      |             |            |            |       |       |
|      |             |            |            |       |       |
|      |             |            |            |       |       |
|      |             |            |            |       |       |

Date : _____  Start time : _____  Session No : _____

Client Name : _____  Topic : _____

| Session Talking Points : | Key Points from Previous Session : |
|---|---|
| ✔ _____ | ✔ _____ |
| ✔ _____ | ✔ _____ |
| ✔ _____ | ✔ _____ |
| ✔ _____ | ✔ _____ |

Notes : _____

_____

_____

_____

_____

_____

_____

_____

_____

_____

_____

_____

_____

_____

_____

_____

_____

_____

_____

_____

_____

_____

_____

# Extra Notes :

_____
_____
_____
_____
_____
_____
_____

## Client Actions :

✔ _____     ✔ _____
✔ _____     ✔ _____
✔ _____     ✔ _____

## Concerns :                ## Recommendations :

✔ _____     ✔ _____
✔ _____     ✔ _____
✔ _____     ✔ _____

## Overall Comments :

_____
_____
_____

## Next Session Talking Points :

✔ _____     ✔ _____
✔ _____     ✔ _____
✔ _____     ✔ _____

Next Session Date : _____     End Time : _____

Date : _____     Start time : _____     Session No : _____

Client Name : _____          Topic : _____

### Session Talking Points :

✓ _____

✓ _____

✓ _____

✓ _____

### Key Points from Previous Session :

✓ _____

✓ _____

✓ _____

✓ _____

### Notes : _____

_____

_____

_____

_____

_____

_____

_____

_____

_____

_____

_____

_____

_____

_____

_____

_____

_____

_____

_____

_____

# Extra Notes :

_____
_____
_____
_____
_____
_____
_____

## Client Actions :

✔ _____  ✔ _____
✔ _____  ✔ _____
✔ _____  ✔ _____

## Concerns :                      ## Recommendations :

✔ _____  ✔ _____
✔ _____  ✔ _____
✔ _____  ✔ _____

## Overall Comments :

_____
_____
_____
_____

## Next Session Talking Points :

✔ _____  ✔ _____
✔ _____  ✔ _____
✔ _____  ✔ _____

Next Session Date : _____   End Time : _____

Date : _____  Start time : _____  Session No : _____

Client Name : _____  Topic : _____

| Session Talking Points : | Key Points from Previous Session : |
|---|---|
| ✔ _____ | ✔ _____ |
| ✔ _____ | ✔ _____ |
| ✔ _____ | ✔ _____ |
| ✔ _____ | ✔ _____ |

Notes : _____

_____

_____

_____

_____

_____

_____

_____

_____

_____

_____

_____

_____

_____

_____

_____

_____

_____

_____

_____

_____

_____

# Extra Notes :

_____
_____
_____
_____
_____
_____
_____

## Client Actions :

✔ _____    ✔ _____
✔ _____    ✔ _____
✔ _____    ✔ _____

## Concerns :                 ## Recommendations :

✔ _____    ✔ _____
✔ _____    ✔ _____
✔ _____    ✔ _____

## Overall Comments :

_____
_____
_____
_____

## Next Session Talking Points :

✔ _____    ✔ _____
✔ _____    ✔ _____
✔ _____    ✔ _____

Next Session Date : _____    End Time : _____

Date : _____     Start time : _____     Session No : _____
Client Name : _____          Topic : _____

Session Talking Points :          Key Points from Previous Session :

✓ _____          ✓ _____

✓ _____          ✓ _____

✓ _____          ✓ _____

✓ _____          ✓ _____

Notes : _____

_____

_____

_____

_____

_____

_____

_____

_____

_____

_____

_____

_____

_____

_____

_____

_____

_____

_____

_____

# Extra Notes :

_____
_____
_____
_____
_____
_____
_____
_____

## Client Actions :

✔ _____     ✔ _____
✔ _____     ✔ _____
✔ _____     ✔ _____

## Concerns :                 ## Recommendations :

✔ _____     ✔ _____
✔ _____     ✔ _____
✔ _____     ✔ _____

## Overall Comments :

_____
_____
_____

## Next Session Talking Points :

✔ _____     ✔ _____
✔ _____     ✔ _____
✔ _____     ✔ _____

Next Session Date : _____     End Time : _____

Date : _____    Start time : _____    Session No : _____

Client Name : _____                Topic : _____

---

### Session Talking Points :

✔ _____

✔ _____

✔ _____

✔ _____

### Key Points from Previous Session :

✔ _____

✔ _____

✔ _____

✔ _____

Notes : _____

_____

_____

_____

_____

_____

_____

_____

_____

_____

_____

_____

_____

_____

_____

_____

_____

_____

_____

_____

_____

# Extra Notes :

_____
_____
_____
_____
_____
_____
_____
_____

## Client Actions :

✔ _____     ✔ _____
✔ _____     ✔ _____
✔ _____     ✔ _____

## Concerns :                    ## Recommendations :

✔ _____     ✔ _____
✔ _____     ✔ _____
✔ _____     ✔ _____

## Overall Comments :

_____
_____
_____
_____

## Next Session Talking Points :

✔ _____     ✔ _____
✔ _____     ✔ _____
✔ _____     ✔ _____

Next Session Date : _____     End Time : _____

Date : _____    Start time : _____    Session No : _____

Client Name : _____                    Topic : _____

## Session Talking Points :

✔ _____

✔ _____

✔ _____

✔ _____

## Key Points from Previous Session :

✔ _____

✔ _____

✔ _____

✔ _____

## Notes :

_____

_____

_____

_____

_____

_____

_____

_____

_____

_____

_____

_____

_____

_____

_____

_____

_____

_____

_____

# Extra Notes :

_____
_____
_____
_____
_____
_____
_____
_____

## Client Actions :

✔ _____    ✔ _____
✔ _____    ✔ _____
✔ _____    ✔ _____

## Concerns :           Recommendations :

✔ _____    ✔ _____
✔ _____    ✔ _____
✔ _____    ✔ _____

## Overall Comments :

_____
_____
_____
_____

## Next Session Talking Points :

✔ _____    ✔ _____
✔ _____    ✔ _____
✔ _____    ✔ _____

Next Session Date : _____    End Time : _____

Date : _____ Start time : _____ Session No : _____

Client Name : _____ Topic : _____

| Session Talking Points : | Key Points from Previous Session : |
|---|---|
| ✔ _____ | ✔ _____ |
| ✔ _____ | ✔ _____ |
| ✔ _____ | ✔ _____ |
| ✔ _____ | ✔ _____ |

Notes :

_____

_____

_____

_____

_____

_____

_____

_____

_____

_____

_____

_____

_____

_____

_____

_____

_____

_____

# Extra Notes :

_____
_____
_____
_____
_____
_____
_____

## Client Actions :

✔ _____     ✔ _____
✔ _____     ✔ _____
✔ _____     ✔ _____

## Concerns :                     Recommendations :

✔ _____     ✔ _____
✔ _____     ✔ _____
✔ _____     ✔ _____

## Overall Comments :

_____
_____
_____
_____

## Next Session Talking Points :

✔ _____     ✔ _____
✔ _____     ✔ _____
✔ _____     ✔ _____

Next Session Date : _____     End Time : _____

Date : _____ Start time : _____ Session No : _____

Client Name : _____ Topic : _____

## Session Talking Points :

✔ _____

✔ _____

✔ _____

✔ _____

## Key Points from Previous Session :

✔ _____

✔ _____

✔ _____

✔ _____

## Notes :

_____

_____

_____

_____

_____

_____

_____

_____

_____

_____

_____

_____

_____

_____

_____

_____

_____

# Extra Notes :

_____
_____
_____
_____
_____
_____
_____
_____

## Client Actions :

✔ _____    ✔ _____
✔ _____    ✔ _____
✔ _____    ✔ _____

## Concerns :                        Recommendations :

✔ _____    ✔ _____
✔ _____    ✔ _____
✔ _____    ✔ _____

## Overall Comments :

_____
_____
_____

## Next Session Talking Points :

✔ _____    ✔ _____
✔ _____    ✔ _____
✔ _____    ✔ _____

Next Session Date : _____    End Time : _____

Date : _____ Start time : _____ Session No : _____

Client Name : _____ Topic : _____

Session Talking Points :

✓ _____

✓ _____

✓ _____

✓ _____

Key Points from Previous Session :

✓ _____

✓ _____

✓ _____

✓ _____

Notes : _____

_____

_____

_____

_____

_____

_____

_____

_____

_____

_____

_____

_____

_____

_____

_____

_____

_____

_____

_____

_____

# Extra Notes :

_____
_____
_____
_____
_____
_____
_____
_____

## Client Actions :

✔ _____  ✔ _____
✔ _____  ✔ _____
✔ _____  ✔ _____

## Concerns :                    ## Recommendations :

✔ _____  ✔ _____
✔ _____  ✔ _____
✔ _____  ✔ _____

## Overall Comments :

_____
_____
_____

## Next Session Talking Points :

✔ _____  ✔ _____
✔ _____  ✔ _____
✔ _____  ✔ _____

Next Session Date : _____  End Time : _____

Date : _____ Start time : _____ Session No : _____

Client Name : _____ Topic : _____

| Session Talking Points : | Key Points from Previous Session : |

✔ _____     ✔ _____

✔ _____     ✔ _____

✔ _____     ✔ _____

✔ _____     ✔ _____

Notes : _____

# Extra Notes :

_____
_____
_____
_____
_____
_____
_____

## Client Actions :

✔ _____    ✔ _____
✔ _____    ✔ _____
✔ _____    ✔ _____

## Concerns :                 ## Recommendations :

✔ _____    ✔ _____
✔ _____    ✔ _____
✔ _____    ✔ _____

## Overall Comments :

_____
_____
_____

## Next Session Talking Points :

✔ _____    ✔ _____
✔ _____    ✔ _____
✔ _____    ✔ _____

Next Session Date : _____    End Time : _____

Date : _____   Start time : _____   Session No : _____

Client Name : _____   Topic : _____

_____

<table>
<tr><td>Session Talking Points :</td><td>Key Points from Previous Session :</td></tr>
<tr><td>✔ _____</td><td>✔ _____</td></tr>
<tr><td>✔ _____</td><td>✔ _____</td></tr>
<tr><td>✔ _____</td><td>✔ _____</td></tr>
<tr><td>✔ _____</td><td>✔ _____</td></tr>
</table>

Notes : _____

_____

_____

_____

_____

_____

_____

_____

_____

_____

_____

_____

_____

_____

_____

_____

_____

## Extra Notes :

_____
_____
_____
_____
_____
_____
_____

## Client Actions :

✔ _____     ✔ _____
✔ _____     ✔ _____
✔ _____     ✔ _____

## Concerns :                          ## Recommendations :

✔ _____     ✔ _____
✔ _____     ✔ _____
✔ _____     ✔ _____

## Overall Comments :

_____
_____
_____

## Next Session Talking Points :

✔ _____     ✔ _____
✔ _____     ✔ _____
✔ _____     ✔ _____

Next Session Date : _____     End Time : _____

Date : _____ Start time : _____ Session No : _____

Client Name : _____ Topic : _____

| Session Talking Points : | Key Points from Previous Session : |
|---|---|
| ✔ _____ | ✔ _____ |
| ✔ _____ | ✔ _____ |
| ✔ _____ | ✔ _____ |
| ✔ _____ | ✔ _____ |

Notes : _____

_____

_____

_____

_____

_____

_____

_____

_____

_____

_____

_____

_____

_____

_____

_____

_____

_____

_____

# Extra Notes :

_____
_____
_____
_____
_____
_____
_____
_____

## Client Actions :

✔ _____    ✔ _____
✔ _____    ✔ _____
✔ _____    ✔ _____

## Concerns :                    Recommendations :

✔ _____    ✔ _____
✔ _____    ✔ _____
✔ _____    ✔ _____

## Overall Comments :

_____
_____
_____
_____

## Next Session Talking Points :

✔ _____    ✔ _____
✔ _____    ✔ _____
✔ _____    ✔ _____

Next Session Date : _____    End Time : _____

Date : _____ Start time : _____ Session No : _____

Client Name : _____ Topic : _____

| Session Talking Points : | Key Points from Previous Session : |
|---|---|
| ✔ _____ | ✔ _____ |
| ✔ _____ | ✔ _____ |
| ✔ _____ | ✔ _____ |
| ✔ _____ | ✔ _____ |

Notes : _____

_____

_____

_____

_____

_____

_____

_____

_____

_____

_____

_____

_____

_____

_____

_____

_____

_____

_____

_____

_____

Extra Notes :

_____
_____
_____
_____
_____
_____
_____
_____

Client Actions :

✔ _____   ✔ _____
✔ _____   ✔ _____
✔ _____   ✔ _____

Concerns :                   Recommendations :

✔ _____   ✔ _____
✔ _____   ✔ _____
✔ _____   ✔ _____

Overall Comments :

_____
_____
_____

Next Session Talking Points :

✔ _____   ✔ _____
✔ _____   ✔ _____
✔ _____   ✔ _____

Next Session Date : _____   End Time : _____

26

Date : _____  Start time : _____  Session No : _____

Client Name : _____  Topic : _____

Session Talking Points :              Key Points from Previous Session :

✔ _____        ✔ _____

✔ _____        ✔ _____

✔ _____        ✔ _____

✔ _____        ✔ _____

Notes : _____

_____

_____

_____

_____

_____

_____

_____

_____

_____

_____

_____

_____

_____

_____

_____

_____

_____

_____

# Extra Notes :

_____
_____
_____
_____
_____
_____

## Client Actions :

✔ _____    ✔ _____
✔ _____    ✔ _____
✔ _____    ✔ _____

## Concerns :                    ## Recommendations :

✔ _____    ✔ _____
✔ _____    ✔ _____
✔ _____    ✔ _____

## Overall Comments :

_____
_____
_____

## Next Session Talking Points :

✔ _____    ✔ _____
✔ _____    ✔ _____
✔ _____    ✔ _____

Next Session Date : _____    End Time : _____

Date : _____ Start time : _____ Session No : _____

Client Name : _____ Topic : _____

Session Talking Points :

✔ _____

✔ _____

✔ _____

✔ _____

Key Points from Previous Session :

✔ _____

✔ _____

✔ _____

✔ _____

Notes : _____

_____

_____

_____

_____

_____

_____

_____

_____

_____

_____

_____

_____

_____

_____

_____

_____

_____

_____

_____

_____

_____

# Extra Notes :

_____
_____
_____
_____
_____
_____
_____

## Client Actions :

✔ _____    ✔ _____
✔ _____    ✔ _____
✔ _____    ✔ _____

## Concerns :                    ## Recommendations :

✔ _____    ✔ _____
✔ _____    ✔ _____
✔ _____    ✔ _____

## Overall Comments :

_____
_____
_____
_____

## Next Session Talking Points :

✔ _____    ✔ _____
✔ _____    ✔ _____
✔ _____    ✔ _____

Next Session Date : _____    End Time : _____

Date : _____  Start time : _____  Session No : _____

Client Name : _____  Topic : _____

Session Talking Points :     Key Points from Previous Session :

✓ _____     ✓ _____

✓ _____     ✓ _____

✓ _____     ✓ _____

✓ _____     ✓ _____

Notes :

Extra Notes :

Client Actions :

✔ _____    ✔ _____
✔ _____    ✔ _____
✔ _____    ✔ _____

Concerns :                    Recommendations :

✔ _____    ✔ _____
✔ _____    ✔ _____
✔ _____    ✔ _____

Overall Comments :

Next Session Talking Points :

✔ _____    ✔ _____
✔ _____    ✔ _____
✔ _____    ✔ _____

Next Session Date : _____    End Time : _____

Date : _____  Start time : _____  Session No : _____
Client Name : _____  Topic : _____

Session Talking Points :

✓ _____
✓ _____
✓ _____
✓ _____

Key Points from Previous Session :

✓ _____
✓ _____
✓ _____
✓ _____

Notes : _____

_____
_____
_____
_____
_____
_____
_____
_____
_____
_____
_____
_____
_____
_____
_____
_____
_____
_____
_____

# Extra Notes :

_____

_____

_____

_____

_____

_____

## Client Actions :

✔ _____  ✔ _____

✔ _____  ✔ _____

✔ _____  ✔ _____

## Concerns :                    Recommendations :

✔ _____  ✔ _____

✔ _____  ✔ _____

✔ _____  ✔ _____

## Overall Comments :

_____

_____

_____

## Next Session Talking Points :

✔ _____  ✔ _____

✔ _____  ✔ _____

✔ _____  ✔ _____

Next Session Date : _____  End Time : _____

Date : _____ Start time : _____ Session No : _____

Client Name : _____ Topic : _____

Session Talking Points :

✓ _____

✓ _____

✓ _____

✓ _____

Key Points from Previous Session :

✓ _____

✓ _____

✓ _____

✓ _____

Notes :

# Extra Notes :

_____
_____
_____
_____
_____
_____
_____

## Client Actions :

✔ _____  ✔ _____
✔ _____  ✔ _____
✔ _____  ✔ _____

## Concerns :                    ## Recommendations :

✔ _____  ✔ _____
✔ _____  ✔ _____
✔ _____  ✔ _____

## Overall Comments :

_____
_____
_____
_____

## Next Session Talking Points :

✔ _____  ✔ _____
✔ _____  ✔ _____
✔ _____  ✔ _____

Next Session Date : _____    End Time : _____

Date : _____  Start time : _____  Session No : _____

Client Name : _____  Topic : _____

Session Talking Points :               Key Points from Previous Session :

✓ _____        ✓ _____

✓ _____        ✓ _____

✓ _____        ✓ _____

✓ _____        ✓ _____

Notes : _____

# Extra Notes :

## Client Actions :

✔ _____  ✔ _____

✔ _____  ✔ _____

✔ _____  ✔ _____

### Concerns :

✔ _____

✔ _____

✔ _____

### Recommendations :

✔ _____

✔ _____

✔ _____

## Overall Comments :

## Next Session Talking Points :

✔ _____  ✔ _____

✔ _____  ✔ _____

✔ _____  ✔ _____

Next Session Date : _____  End Time : _____

Date : _____ Start time : _____ Session No : _____

Client Name : _____ Topic : _____

Session Talking Points :                Key Points from Previous Session :

✔ _____          ✔ _____

✔ _____          ✔ _____

✔ _____          ✔ _____

✔ _____          ✔ _____

Notes : _____

_____

_____

_____

_____

_____

_____

_____

_____

_____

_____

_____

_____

_____

_____

_____

_____

_____

_____

# Extra Notes :

_____
_____
_____
_____
_____
_____
_____

## Client Actions :

✔ _____    ✔ _____
✔ _____    ✔ _____
✔ _____    ✔ _____

## Concerns :                    Recommendations :

✔ _____    ✔ _____
✔ _____    ✔ _____
✔ _____    ✔ _____

## Overall Comments :

_____
_____
_____

## Next Session Talking Points :

✔ _____    ✔ _____
✔ _____    ✔ _____
✔ _____    ✔ _____

Next Session Date : _____    End Time : _____

Date : _____   Start time : _____   Session No : _____

Client Name : _____   Topic : _____

---

Session Talking Points :

✔ _____

✔ _____

✔ _____

✔ _____

Key Points from Previous Session :

✔ _____

✔ _____

✔ _____

✔ _____

Notes : _____

_____

_____

_____

_____

_____

_____

_____

_____

_____

_____

_____

_____

_____

_____

_____

_____

_____

_____

# Extra Notes :

_____
_____
_____
_____
_____
_____

## Client Actions :

✔ _____       ✔ _____
✔ _____       ✔ _____
✔ _____       ✔ _____

### Concerns :                    ### Recommendations :

✔ _____       ✔ _____
✔ _____       ✔ _____
✔ _____       ✔ _____

## Overall Comments :

_____
_____
_____

## Next Session Talking Points :

✔ _____       ✔ _____
✔ _____       ✔ _____
✔ _____       ✔ _____

Next Session Date : _____    End Time : _____

Date : _____ Start time : _____ Session No : _____

Client Name : _____ Topic : _____

## Session Talking Points :

✔ _____

✔ _____

✔ _____

✔ _____

## Key Points from Previous Session :

✔ _____

✔ _____

✔ _____

✔ _____

## Notes : _____

_____

_____

_____

_____

_____

_____

_____

_____

_____

_____

_____

_____

_____

_____

_____

_____

_____

_____

# Extra Notes :

_____
_____
_____
_____
_____
_____
_____
_____
_____

## Client Actions :

✔ _____    ✔ _____
✔ _____    ✔ _____
✔ _____    ✔ _____

### Concerns :                    ### Recommendations :

✔ _____    ✔ _____
✔ _____    ✔ _____
✔ _____    ✔ _____

## Overall Comments :

_____
_____
_____
_____

## Next Session Talking Points :

✔ _____    ✔ _____
✔ _____    ✔ _____
✔ _____    ✔ _____

Next Session Date : _____    End Time : _____

Date : _____ Start time : _____ Session No : _____
Client Name : _____ Topic : _____

## Session Talking Points :
- ✔ _____
- ✔ _____
- ✔ _____
- ✔ _____

## Key Points from Previous Session :
- ✔ _____
- ✔ _____
- ✔ _____
- ✔ _____

Notes : _____

_____

_____

_____

_____

_____

_____

_____

_____

_____

_____

_____

_____

_____

_____

_____

_____

_____

_____

_____

# Extra Notes :

## Client Actions :

✔ _____  ✔ _____
✔ _____  ✔ _____
✔ _____  ✔ _____

## Concerns :

✔ _____
✔ _____
✔ _____

## Recommendations :

✔ _____
✔ _____
✔ _____

## Overall Comments :

## Next Session Talking Points :

✔ _____  ✔ _____
✔ _____  ✔ _____
✔ _____  ✔ _____

Next Session Date : _____     End Time : _____

Date : _____    Start time : _____    Session No : _____

Client Name : _____    Topic : _____

## Session Talking Points :

- ✓ _____
- ✓ _____
- ✓ _____
- ✓ _____

## Key Points from Previous Session :

- ✓ _____
- ✓ _____
- ✓ _____
- ✓ _____

## Notes :

_____

_____

_____

_____

_____

_____

_____

_____

_____

_____

_____

_____

_____

_____

_____

_____

_____

_____

# Extra Notes :

_____
_____
_____
_____
_____
_____
_____

## Client Actions :

✔ _____     ✔ _____
✔ _____     ✔ _____
✔ _____     ✔ _____

## Concerns :                    Recommendations :

✔ _____     ✔ _____
✔ _____     ✔ _____
✔ _____     ✔ _____

## Overall Comments :

_____
_____
_____

## Next Session Talking Points :

✔ _____     ✔ _____
✔ _____     ✔ _____
✔ _____     ✔ _____

Next Session Date : _____     End Time : _____

Date : _____ Start time : _____ Session No : _____

Client Name : _____ Topic : _____

Session Talking Points :

✓ _____

✓ _____

✓ _____

✓ _____

Key Points from Previous Session :

✓ _____

✓ _____

✓ _____

✓ _____

Notes :

# Extra Notes :

_____
_____
_____
_____
_____
_____
_____

## Client Actions :

✔ _____        ✔ _____
✔ _____        ✔ _____
✔ _____        ✔ _____

## Concerns :                    Recommendations :

✔ _____        ✔ _____
✔ _____        ✔ _____
✔ _____        ✔ _____

## Overall Comments :

_____
_____
_____

## Next Session Talking Points :

✔ _____        ✔ _____
✔ _____        ✔ _____
✔ _____        ✔ _____

Next Session Date : _____        End Time : _____

Date : _____  Start time : _____  Session No : _____

Client Name : _____  Topic : _____

| Session Talking Points : | Key Points from Previous Session : |
|---|---|
| ✓ _____ | ✓ _____ |
| ✓ _____ | ✓ _____ |
| ✓ _____ | ✓ _____ |
| ✓ _____ | ✓ _____ |

Notes : _____

_____

_____

_____

_____

_____

_____

_____

_____

_____

_____

_____

_____

_____

_____

_____

_____

# Extra Notes :

_____
_____
_____
_____
_____
_____
_____

## Client Actions :

✔ _____     ✔ _____
✔ _____     ✔ _____
✔ _____     ✔ _____

## Concerns :                    ## Recommendations :

✔ _____     ✔ _____
✔ _____     ✔ _____
✔ _____     ✔ _____

## Overall Comments :

_____
_____
_____
_____

## Next Session Talking Points :

✔ _____     ✔ _____
✔ _____     ✔ _____
✔ _____     ✔ _____

Next Session Date : _____     End Time : _____

Date : _____ Start time : _____ Session No : _____

Client Name : _____ Topic : _____

| Session Talking Points : | Key Points from Previous Session : |
|---|---|
| ✔ _____ | ✔ _____ |
| ✔ _____ | ✔ _____ |
| ✔ _____ | ✔ _____ |
| ✔ _____ | ✔ _____ |

Notes : _____

_____

_____

_____

_____

_____

_____

_____

_____

_____

_____

_____

_____

_____

_____

_____

_____

_____

_____

# Extra Notes :

_____
_____
_____
_____
_____
_____
_____
_____

## Client Actions :

✔ _____      ✔ _____
✔ _____      ✔ _____
✔ _____      ✔ _____

## Concerns :                    ## Recommendations :

✔ _____      ✔ _____
✔ _____      ✔ _____
✔ _____      ✔ _____

## Overall Comments :

_____
_____
_____
_____

## Next Session Talking Points :

✔ _____      ✔ _____
✔ _____      ✔ _____
✔ _____      ✔ _____

Next Session Date : _____      End Time : _____

Date : _____ Start time : _____ Session No : _____

Client Name : _____ Topic : _____

_____

Session Talking Points :  Key Points from Previous Session :

✔ _____  ✔ _____

✔ _____  ✔ _____

✔ _____  ✔ _____

✔ _____  ✔ _____

Notes :

_____

_____

_____

_____

_____

_____

_____

_____

_____

_____

_____

_____

_____

_____

_____

_____

_____

# Extra Notes :

_____
_____
_____
_____
_____
_____
_____
_____

## Client Actions :

✓ _____    ✓ _____
✓ _____    ✓ _____
✓ _____    ✓ _____

## Concerns :                    ## Recommendations :

✓ _____    ✓ _____
✓ _____    ✓ _____
✓ _____    ✓ _____

## Overall Comments :

_____
_____
_____

## Next Session Talking Points :

✓ _____    ✓ _____
✓ _____    ✓ _____
✓ _____    ✓ _____

Next Session Date : _____    End Time : _____

Date : _____ Start time : _____ Session No : _____

Client Name : _____ Topic : _____

| Session Talking Points : | Key Points from Previous Session : |
|---|---|
| ✓ _____ | ✓ _____ |
| ✓ _____ | ✓ _____ |
| ✓ _____ | ✓ _____ |
| ✓ _____ | ✓ _____ |

Notes : _____

_____

_____

_____

_____

_____

_____

_____

_____

_____

_____

_____

_____

_____

_____

_____

_____

_____

_____

_____

# Extra Notes :

_____
_____
_____
_____
_____
_____
_____

## Client Actions :

✓ _____     ✓ _____
✓ _____     ✓ _____
✓ _____     ✓ _____

## Concerns :                    Recommendations :

✓ _____     ✓ _____
✓ _____     ✓ _____
✓ _____     ✓ _____

## Overall Comments :

_____
_____
_____

## Next Session Talking Points :

✓ _____     ✓ _____
✓ _____     ✓ _____
✓ _____     ✓ _____

Next Session Date : _____     End Time : _____

Date : _____ Start time : _____ Session No : _____

Client Name : _____ Topic : _____

### Session Talking Points :

✓ _____

✓ _____

✓ _____

✓ _____

### Key Points from Previous Session :

✓ _____

✓ _____

✓ _____

✓ _____

Notes :

_____

_____

_____

_____

_____

_____

_____

_____

_____

_____

_____

_____

_____

_____

_____

_____

## Extra Notes :

_____
_____
_____
_____
_____
_____
_____

## Client Actions :

✔ _____     ✔ _____
✔ _____     ✔ _____
✔ _____     ✔ _____

## Concerns :                        Recommendations :

✔ _____     ✔ _____
✔ _____     ✔ _____
✔ _____     ✔ _____

## Overall Comments :

_____
_____
_____

## Next Session Talking Points :

✔ _____     ✔ _____
✔ _____     ✔ _____
✔ _____     ✔ _____

Next Session Date : _____     End Time : _____

Date : _____ Start time : _____ Session No : _____

Client Name : _____ Topic : _____

## Session Talking Points :

✓ _____
✓ _____
✓ _____
✓ _____

## Key Points from Previous Session :

✓ _____
✓ _____
✓ _____
✓ _____

## Notes :

_____
_____
_____
_____
_____
_____
_____
_____
_____
_____
_____
_____
_____
_____
_____
_____
_____
_____
_____
_____

# Extra Notes :

_____
_____
_____
_____
_____
_____

## Client Actions :

✔ _____    ✔ _____
✔ _____    ✔ _____
✔ _____    ✔ _____

## Concerns :                 ## Recommendations :

✔ _____    ✔ _____
✔ _____    ✔ _____
✔ _____    ✔ _____

## Overall Comments :

_____
_____
_____

## Next Session Talking Points :

✔ _____    ✔ _____
✔ _____    ✔ _____
✔ _____    ✔ _____

Next Session Date : _____    End Time : _____

Date : _____ Start time : _____ Session No : _____

Client Name : _____ Topic : _____

Session Talking Points :

✔ _____
✔ _____
✔ _____
✔ _____

Key Points from Previous Session :

✔ _____
✔ _____
✔ _____
✔ _____

Notes :

_____
_____
_____
_____
_____
_____
_____
_____
_____
_____
_____
_____
_____
_____
_____
_____
_____
_____

Extra Notes :

Client Actions :

✔ _____    ✔ _____
✔ _____    ✔ _____
✔ _____    ✔ _____

Concerns :                   Recommendations :

✔ _____    ✔ _____
✔ _____    ✔ _____
✔ _____    ✔ _____

Overall Comments :

Next Session Talking Points :

✔ _____    ✔ _____
✔ _____    ✔ _____
✔ _____    ✔ _____

Next Session Date : _____    End Time : _____

Date : _____    Start time : _____    Session No : _____

Client Name : _____    Topic : _____

---

Session Talking Points :

✔ _____

✔ _____

✔ _____

✔ _____

Key Points from Previous Session :

✔ _____

✔ _____

✔ _____

✔ _____

Notes : _____

_____

_____

_____

_____

_____

_____

_____

_____

_____

_____

_____

_____

_____

_____

_____

_____

_____

_____

_____

_____

# Extra Notes :

_____
_____
_____
_____
_____
_____
_____

## Client Actions :

✓ _____     ✓ _____
✓ _____     ✓ _____
✓ _____     ✓ _____

## Concerns :                  ## Recommendations :

✓ _____     ✓ _____
✓ _____     ✓ _____
✓ _____     ✓ _____

## Overall Comments :

_____
_____
_____

## Next Session Talking Points :

✓ _____     ✓ _____
✓ _____     ✓ _____
✓ _____     ✓ _____

Next Session Date : _____     End Time : _____

Date : _____  Start time : _____  Session No : _____

Client Name : _____  Topic : _____

Session Talking Points :

✓ _____
✓ _____
✓ _____
✓ _____

Key Points from Previous Session :

✓ _____
✓ _____
✓ _____
✓ _____

Notes : _____

_____
_____
_____
_____
_____
_____
_____
_____
_____
_____
_____
_____
_____
_____
_____
_____
_____
_____
_____

# Extra Notes :

## Client Actions :

✓ _____  ✓ _____

✓ _____  ✓ _____

✓ _____  ✓ _____

## Concerns :                      ## Recommendations :

✓ _____  ✓ _____

✓ _____  ✓ _____

✓ _____  ✓ _____

## Overall Comments :

## Next Session Talking Points :

✓ _____  ✓ _____

✓ _____  ✓ _____

✓ _____  ✓ _____

Next Session Date : _____        End Time : _____

Date : _____ Start time : _____ Session No : _____

Client Name : _____ Topic : _____

### Session Talking Points :

✓ _____
✓ _____
✓ _____
✓ _____

### Key Points from Previous Session :

✓ _____
✓ _____
✓ _____
✓ _____

Notes : _____

_____
_____
_____
_____
_____
_____
_____
_____
_____
_____
_____
_____
_____
_____
_____
_____
_____
_____
_____
_____
_____

## Extra Notes :

_____
_____
_____
_____
_____
_____

## Client Actions :

✔ _____  ✔ _____

✔ _____  ✔ _____

✔ _____  ✔ _____

## Concerns :                 ## Recommendations :

✔ _____  ✔ _____

✔ _____  ✔ _____

✔ _____  ✔ _____

## Overall Comments :

_____
_____
_____

## Next Session Talking Points :

✔ _____  ✔ _____

✔ _____  ✔ _____

✔ _____  ✔ _____

Next Session Date : _____  End Time : _____

Date : _____ Start time : _____ Session No : _____

Client Name : _____ Topic : _____

## Session Talking Points :

- ✔ _____
- ✔ _____
- ✔ _____
- ✔ _____

## Key Points from Previous Session :

- ✔ _____
- ✔ _____
- ✔ _____
- ✔ _____

Notes : _____

_____

_____

_____

_____

_____

_____

_____

_____

_____

_____

_____

_____

_____

_____

_____

_____

_____

_____

_____

# Extra Notes :

_____
_____
_____
_____
_____
_____
_____

## Client Actions :

✔ _____    ✔ _____
✔ _____    ✔ _____
✔ _____    ✔ _____

## Concerns :                    ## Recommendations :

✔ _____    ✔ _____
✔ _____    ✔ _____
✔ _____    ✔ _____

## Overall Comments :

_____
_____
_____

## Next Session Talking Points :

✔ _____    ✔ _____
✔ _____    ✔ _____
✔ _____    ✔ _____

Next Session Date : _____    End Time : _____

Date : _____ Start time : _____ Session No : _____

Client Name : _____ Topic : _____

Session Talking Points :

✓ _____

✓ _____

✓ _____

✓ _____

Key Points from Previous Session :

✓ _____

✓ _____

✓ _____

✓ _____

Notes : _____

_____

_____

_____

_____

_____

_____

_____

_____

_____

_____

_____

_____

_____

_____

_____

_____

_____

_____

_____

# Extra Notes :

_____
_____
_____
_____
_____
_____
_____
_____

## Client Actions :

✔ _____    ✔ _____
✔ _____    ✔ _____
✔ _____    ✔ _____

## Concerns :                Recommendations :

✔ _____    ✔ _____
✔ _____    ✔ _____
✔ _____    ✔ _____

## Overall Comments :

_____
_____
_____

## Next Session Talking Points :

✔ _____    ✔ _____
✔ _____    ✔ _____
✔ _____    ✔ _____

Next Session Date : _____    End Time : _____

Date : _____ Start time : _____ Session No : _____

Client Name : _____ Topic : _____

Session Talking Points :

✔ _____

✔ _____

✔ _____

✔ _____

Key Points from Previous Session :

✔ _____

✔ _____

✔ _____

✔ _____

Notes : _____

_____

_____

_____

_____

_____

_____

_____

_____

_____

_____

_____

_____

_____

_____

_____

_____

_____

_____

_____

_____

_____

_____

## Extra Notes :

_____
_____
_____
_____
_____
_____
_____

## Client Actions :

✔ _____    ✔ _____
✔ _____    ✔ _____
✔ _____    ✔ _____

## Concerns :                          ## Recommendations :

✔ _____    ✔ _____
✔ _____    ✔ _____
✔ _____    ✔ _____

## Overall Comments :

_____
_____
_____

## Next Session Talking Points :

✔ _____    ✔ _____
✔ _____    ✔ _____
✔ _____    ✔ _____

Next Session Date : _____    End Time : _____

Date : _____  Start time : _____  Session No : _____

Client Name : _____  Topic : _____

Session Talking Points :          Key Points from Previous Session :

✔ _____                     ✔ _____

✔ _____                     ✔ _____

✔ _____                     ✔ _____

✔ _____                     ✔ _____

Notes :

# Extra Notes :

_____
_____
_____
_____
_____
_____
_____

## Client Actions :

✓ _____     ✓ _____
✓ _____     ✓ _____
✓ _____     ✓ _____

## Concerns :                 Recommendations :

✓ _____     ✓ _____
✓ _____     ✓ _____
✓ _____     ✓ _____

## Overall Comments :

_____
_____
_____

## Next Session Talking Points :

✓ _____     ✓ _____
✓ _____     ✓ _____
✓ _____     ✓ _____

Next Session Date : _____   End Time : _____

Date : _____ Start time : _____ Session No : _____

Client Name : _____ Topic : _____

## Session Talking Points :

✔ _____

✔ _____

✔ _____

✔ _____

## Key Points from Previous Session :

✔ _____

✔ _____

✔ _____

✔ _____

## Notes :

_____

_____

_____

_____

_____

_____

_____

_____

_____

_____

_____

_____

_____

_____

_____

_____

_____

_____

# Extra Notes :

_____
_____
_____
_____
_____
_____
_____

## Client Actions :

✔ _____      ✔ _____
✔ _____      ✔ _____
✔ _____      ✔ _____

## Concerns :                 ## Recommendations :

✔ _____      ✔ _____
✔ _____      ✔ _____
✔ _____      ✔ _____

## Overall Comments :

_____
_____
_____

## Next Session Talking Points :

✔ _____      ✔ _____
✔ _____      ✔ _____
✔ _____      ✔ _____

Next Session Date : _____      End Time : _____

Date : _____ Start time : _____ Session No : _____

Client Name : _____ Topic : _____

Session Talking Points :      Key Points from Previous Session :

✓ _____     ✓ _____

✓ _____     ✓ _____

✓ _____     ✓ _____

✓ _____     ✓ _____

Notes : _____

_____

_____

_____

_____

_____

_____

_____

_____

_____

_____

_____

_____

_____

_____

_____

_____

_____

_____

_____

_____

_____

_____

# Extra Notes :

## Client Actions :

✔   ✔

✔   ✔

✔   ✔

## Concerns :

## Recommendations :

✔   ✔

✔   ✔

✔   ✔

## Overall Comments :

## Next Session Talking Points :

✔   ✔

✔   ✔

✔   ✔

Next Session Date :   End Time :

Date : _____ Start time : _____ Session No : _____
Client Name : _____ Topic : _____

Session Talking Points :              Key Points from Previous Session :

✔ _____          ✔ _____

✔ _____          ✔ _____

✔ _____          ✔ _____

✔ _____          ✔ _____

Notes : _____

_____

_____

_____

_____

_____

_____

_____

_____

_____

_____

_____

_____

_____

_____

_____

_____

_____

_____

# Extra Notes :

_____
_____
_____
_____
_____
_____
_____

## Client Actions :

✔ _____     ✔ _____
✔ _____     ✔ _____
✔ _____     ✔ _____

## Concerns :                    ## Recommendations :

✔ _____     ✔ _____
✔ _____     ✔ _____
✔ _____     ✔ _____

## Overall Comments :

_____
_____
_____

## Next Session Talking Points :

✔ _____     ✔ _____
✔ _____     ✔ _____
✔ _____     ✔ _____

Next Session Date : _____     End Time : _____

Date : _____  Start time : _____  Session No : _____
Client Name : _____  Topic : _____

| Session Talking Points : | Key Points from Previous Session : |
|---|---|
| ✔ _____ | ✔ _____ |
| ✔ _____ | ✔ _____ |
| ✔ _____ | ✔ _____ |
| ✔ _____ | ✔ _____ |

Notes :

_____
_____
_____
_____
_____
_____
_____
_____
_____
_____
_____
_____
_____
_____
_____
_____
_____
_____
_____

## Extra Notes :

_____
_____
_____
_____
_____
_____
_____

## Client Actions :

✔ _____    ✔ _____
✔ _____    ✔ _____
✔ _____    ✔ _____

## Concerns :                ## Recommendations :

✔ _____    ✔ _____
✔ _____    ✔ _____
✔ _____    ✔ _____

## Overall Comments :

_____
_____
_____

## Next Session Talking Points :

✔ _____    ✔ _____
✔ _____    ✔ _____
✔ _____    ✔ _____

Next Session Date : _____    End Time : _____

Date : _____    Start time : _____    Session No : _____

Client Name : _____    Topic : _____

Session Talking Points :                Key Points from Previous Session :

✓ _____              ✓ _____

✓ _____              ✓ _____

✓ _____              ✓ _____

✓ _____              ✓ _____

Notes : _____

_____

_____

_____

_____

_____

_____

_____

_____

_____

_____

_____

_____

_____

_____

_____

_____

_____

_____

# Extra Notes :

_____
_____
_____
_____
_____
_____
_____

## Client Actions :

✔ _____     ✔ _____
✔ _____     ✔ _____
✔ _____     ✔ _____

## Concerns :                 ## Recommendations :

✔ _____     ✔ _____
✔ _____     ✔ _____
✔ _____     ✔ _____

## Overall Comments :

_____
_____
_____

## Next Session Talking Points :

✔ _____     ✔ _____
✔ _____     ✔ _____
✔ _____     ✔ _____

Next Session Date : _____     End Time : _____

Date : _____  Start time : _____  Session No : _____

Client Name : _____  Topic : _____

Session Talking Points :

✔ _____

✔ _____

✔ _____

✔ _____

Key Points from Previous Session :

✔ _____

✔ _____

✔ _____

✔ _____

Notes : _____

_____

_____

_____

_____

_____

_____

_____

_____

_____

_____

_____

_____

_____

_____

_____

_____

_____

_____

_____

_____

_____

# Extra Notes :

_____
_____
_____
_____
_____
_____
_____

## Client Actions :

✓ _____  ✓ _____
✓ _____  ✓ _____
✓ _____  ✓ _____

## Concerns :                    ## Recommendations :

✓ _____  ✓ _____
✓ _____  ✓ _____
✓ _____  ✓ _____

## Overall Comments :

_____
_____
_____

## Next Session Talking Points :

✓ _____  ✓ _____
✓ _____  ✓ _____
✓ _____  ✓ _____

Next Session Date : _____    End Time : _____

Date : _____ Start time : _____ Session No : _____

Client Name : _____ Topic : _____

## Session Talking Points :

✓ _____

✓ _____

✓ _____

✓ _____

## Key Points from Previous Session :

✓ _____

✓ _____

✓ _____

✓ _____

Notes : _____

_____

_____

_____

_____

_____

_____

_____

_____

_____

_____

_____

_____

_____

_____

_____

_____

_____

_____

## Extra Notes :

_____
_____
_____
_____
_____
_____
_____

## Client Actions :

✓ _____     ✓ _____
✓ _____     ✓ _____
✓ _____     ✓ _____

## Concerns :          Recommendations :

✓ _____     ✓ _____
✓ _____     ✓ _____
✓ _____     ✓ _____

## Overall Comments :

_____
_____
_____

## Next Session Talking Points :

✓ _____     ✓ _____
✓ _____     ✓ _____
✓ _____     ✓ _____

Next Session Date : _____     End Time : _____

Date : _____  Start time : _____  Session No : _____

Client Name : _____  Topic : _____

Session Talking Points :                Key Points from Previous Session :

✓ _____        ✓ _____

✓ _____        ✓ _____

✓ _____        ✓ _____

✓ _____        ✓ _____

Notes : _____

_____

_____

_____

_____

_____

_____

_____

_____

_____

_____

_____

_____

_____

_____

_____

_____

_____

_____

_____

_____

_____

# Extra Notes :

_____
_____
_____
_____
_____
_____
_____
_____

## Client Actions :

✔ _____    ✔ _____
✔ _____    ✔ _____
✔ _____    ✔ _____

## Concerns :                 ## Recommendations :

✔ _____    ✔ _____
✔ _____    ✔ _____
✔ _____    ✔ _____

## Overall Comments :

_____
_____
_____

## Next Session Talking Points :

✔ _____    ✔ _____
✔ _____    ✔ _____
✔ _____    ✔ _____

Next Session Date : _____    End Time : _____

Date : _____ Start time : _____ Session No : _____

Client Name : _____ Topic : _____

Session Talking Points :      Key Points from Previous Session :

✓ _____    ✓ _____

✓ _____    ✓ _____

✓ _____    ✓ _____

✓ _____    ✓ _____

Notes :

# Extra Notes :

_____
_____
_____
_____
_____
_____

## Client Actions :

✔ _____  ✔ _____
✔ _____  ✔ _____
✔ _____  ✔ _____

## Concerns :                    Recommendations :

✔ _____  ✔ _____
✔ _____  ✔ _____
✔ _____  ✔ _____

## Overall Comments :

_____
_____
_____

## Next Session Talking Points :

✔ _____  ✔ _____
✔ _____  ✔ _____
✔ _____  ✔ _____

Next Session Date : _____     End Time : _____

Date : _____  Start time : _____  Session No : _____

Client Name : _____  Topic : _____

## Session Talking Points :

✔ _____

✔ _____

✔ _____

✔ _____

## Key Points from Previous Session :

✔ _____

✔ _____

✔ _____

✔ _____

Notes :

_____

_____

_____

_____

_____

_____

_____

_____

_____

_____

_____

_____

_____

_____

_____

_____

_____

_____

# Extra Notes :

_____
_____
_____
_____
_____
_____

## Client Actions :

✔ _____     ✔ _____
✔ _____     ✔ _____
✔ _____     ✔ _____

## Concerns :                    ## Recommendations :

✔ _____     ✔ _____
✔ _____     ✔ _____
✔ _____     ✔ _____

## Overall Comments :

_____
_____
_____

## Next Session Talking Points :

✔ _____     ✔ _____
✔ _____     ✔ _____
✔ _____     ✔ _____

Next Session Date : _____     End Time : _____

Date : _____ Start time : _____ Session No : _____

Client Name : _____ Topic : _____

Session Talking Points : Key Points from Previous Session :

✔ _____ ✔ _____

✔ _____ ✔ _____

✔ _____ ✔ _____

✔ _____ ✔ _____

Notes : _____

# Extra Notes :

_____
_____
_____
_____
_____
_____
_____
_____

## Client Actions :

✓ _____      ✓ _____
✓ _____      ✓ _____
✓ _____      ✓ _____

## Concerns :                 ## Recommendations :

✓ _____      ✓ _____
✓ _____      ✓ _____
✓ _____      ✓ _____

## Overall Comments :

_____
_____
_____

## Next Session Talking Points :

✓ _____      ✓ _____
✓ _____      ✓ _____
✓ _____      ✓ _____

Next Session Date : _____      End Time : _____

Date : _____  Start time : _____  Session No : _____
Client Name : _____  Topic : _____

|  Session Talking Points : | Key Points from Previous Session : |
|---|---|
| ✔ _____ | ✔ _____ |
| ✔ _____ | ✔ _____ |
| ✔ _____ | ✔ _____ |
| ✔ _____ | ✔ _____ |

Notes : _____

# Extra Notes :

_____
_____
_____
_____
_____
_____
_____
_____

## Client Actions :

✓ _____ ✓ _____
✓ _____ ✓ _____
✓ _____ ✓ _____

## Concerns :                    ## Recommendations :

✓ _____ ✓ _____
✓ _____ ✓ _____
✓ _____ ✓ _____

## Overall Comments :

_____
_____
_____

## Next Session Talking Points :

✓ _____ ✓ _____
✓ _____ ✓ _____
✓ _____ ✓ _____

Next Session Date : _____ End Time : _____

Date : _____　Start time : _____　Session No : _____

Client Name : _____　　　　Topic : _____

_____

Session Talking Points :　　　　Key Points from Previous Session :

✔ _____　　　　✔ _____

✔ _____　　　　✔ _____

✔ _____　　　　✔ _____

✔ _____　　　　✔ _____

Notes : _____

_____

_____

_____

_____

_____

_____

_____

_____

_____

_____

_____

_____

_____

_____

_____

_____

_____

## Extra Notes :

_____
_____
_____
_____
_____
_____

## Client Actions :

✔ _____  ✔ _____

✔ _____  ✔ _____

✔ _____  ✔ _____

## Concerns :                      Recommendations :

✔ _____  ✔ _____

✔ _____  ✔ _____

✔ _____  ✔ _____

## Overall Comments :

_____
_____
_____

## Next Session Talking Points :

✔ _____  ✔ _____

✔ _____  ✔ _____

✔ _____  ✔ _____

Next Session Date : _____  End Time : _____

Date : _____ Start time : _____ Session No : _____

Client Name : _____ Topic : _____

## Session Talking Points :

✓ _____

✓ _____

✓ _____

✓ _____

## Key Points from Previous Session :

✓ _____

✓ _____

✓ _____

✓ _____

Notes :

# Extra Notes :

_____
_____
_____
_____
_____
_____
_____

## Client Actions :

✔ _____    ✔ _____
✔ _____    ✔ _____
✔ _____    ✔ _____

## Concerns :                    ## Recommendations :

✔ _____    ✔ _____
✔ _____    ✔ _____
✔ _____    ✔ _____

## Overall Comments :

_____
_____
_____

## Next Session Talking Points :

✔ _____    ✔ _____
✔ _____    ✔ _____
✔ _____    ✔ _____

Next Session Date : _____    End Time : _____

Date : _____ Start time : _____ Session No : _____

Client Name : _____ Topic : _____

## Session Talking Points :

✔ _____
✔ _____
✔ _____
✔ _____

## Key Points from Previous Session :

✔ _____
✔ _____
✔ _____
✔ _____

## Notes :

_____

_____

_____

_____

_____

_____

_____

_____

_____

_____

_____

_____

_____

_____

_____

_____

_____

_____

_____

_____

_____

_____

Extra Notes :

_____

_____

_____

_____

_____

_____

Client Actions :

✔ _____    ✔ _____

✔ _____    ✔ _____

✔ _____    ✔ _____

Concerns :                        Recommendations :

✔ _____    ✔ _____

✔ _____    ✔ _____

✔ _____    ✔ _____

Overall Comments :

_____

_____

_____

Next Session Talking Points :

✔ _____    ✔ _____

✔ _____    ✔ _____

✔ _____    ✔ _____

Next Session Date : _____    End Time : _____

Date : _____    Start time : _____    Session No : _____
Client Name : _____    Topic : _____

Session Talking Points :              Key Points from Previous Session :

✔ _____                    ✔ _____
✔ _____                    ✔ _____
✔ _____                    ✔ _____
✔ _____                    ✔ _____

Notes :

_____
_____
_____
_____
_____
_____
_____
_____
_____
_____
_____
_____
_____
_____
_____
_____
_____
_____
_____

Extra Notes :

_____
_____
_____
_____
_____
_____
_____

Client Actions :

✔ _____     ✔ _____
✔ _____     ✔ _____
✔ _____     ✔ _____

Concerns :                 Recommendations :

✔ _____     ✔ _____
✔ _____     ✔ _____
✔ _____     ✔ _____

Overall Comments :

_____
_____
_____

Next Session Talking Points :

✔ _____     ✔ _____
✔ _____     ✔ _____
✔ _____     ✔ _____

Next Session Date : _____     End Time : _____

Date : _____  Start time : _____  Session No : _____

Client Name : _____  Topic : _____

_____

Session Talking Points :  Key Points from Previous Session :

✔ _____  ✔ _____

✔ _____  ✔ _____

✔ _____  ✔ _____

✔ _____  ✔ _____

Notes : _____

_____

_____

_____

_____

_____

_____

_____

_____

_____

_____

_____

_____

_____

_____

_____

_____

_____

_____

_____

_____

# Extra Notes :

## Client Actions :

- ✔
- ✔
- ✔

- ✔
- ✔
- ✔

## Concerns :

- ✔
- ✔
- ✔

## Recommendations :

- ✔
- ✔
- ✔

## Overall Comments :

## Next Session Talking Points :

- ✔
- ✔
- ✔

- ✔
- ✔
- ✔

Next Session Date : _____

End Time : _____

Date : _____ Start time : _____ Session No : _____

Client Name : _____ Topic : _____

_____

### Session Talking Points :

✔ _____

✔ _____

✔ _____

✔ _____

### Key Points from Previous Session :

✔ _____

✔ _____

✔ _____

✔ _____

### Notes :

_____

_____

_____

_____

_____

_____

_____

_____

_____

_____

_____

_____

_____

_____

_____

_____

_____

_____

_____

_____

# Extra Notes :

_____
_____
_____
_____
_____
_____
_____

## Client Actions :

✔ _____     ✔ _____
✔ _____     ✔ _____
✔ _____     ✔ _____

## Concerns :                    ## Recommendations :

✔ _____     ✔ _____
✔ _____     ✔ _____
✔ _____     ✔ _____

## Overall Comments :

_____
_____
_____

## Next Session Talking Points :

✔ _____     ✔ _____
✔ _____     ✔ _____
✔ _____     ✔ _____

Next Session Date : _____     End Time : _____

114

Date : _____ Start time : _____ Session No : _____

Client Name : _____ Topic : _____

## Session Talking Points :

✓ _____

✓ _____

✓ _____

✓ _____

## Key Points from Previous Session :

✓ _____

✓ _____

✓ _____

✓ _____

Notes : _____

_____

_____

_____

_____

_____

_____

_____

_____

_____

_____

_____

_____

_____

_____

_____

_____

_____

_____

# Extra Notes :

## Client Actions :

- ✔
- ✔
- ✔

- ✔
- ✔
- ✔

## Concerns :

- ✔
- ✔
- ✔

## Recommendations :

- ✔
- ✔
- ✔

## Overall Comments :

## Next Session Talking Points :

- ✔
- ✔
- ✔

- ✔
- ✔
- ✔

Next Session Date :

End Time :

Made in the USA
Middletown, DE
13 April 2023

28788254R00071